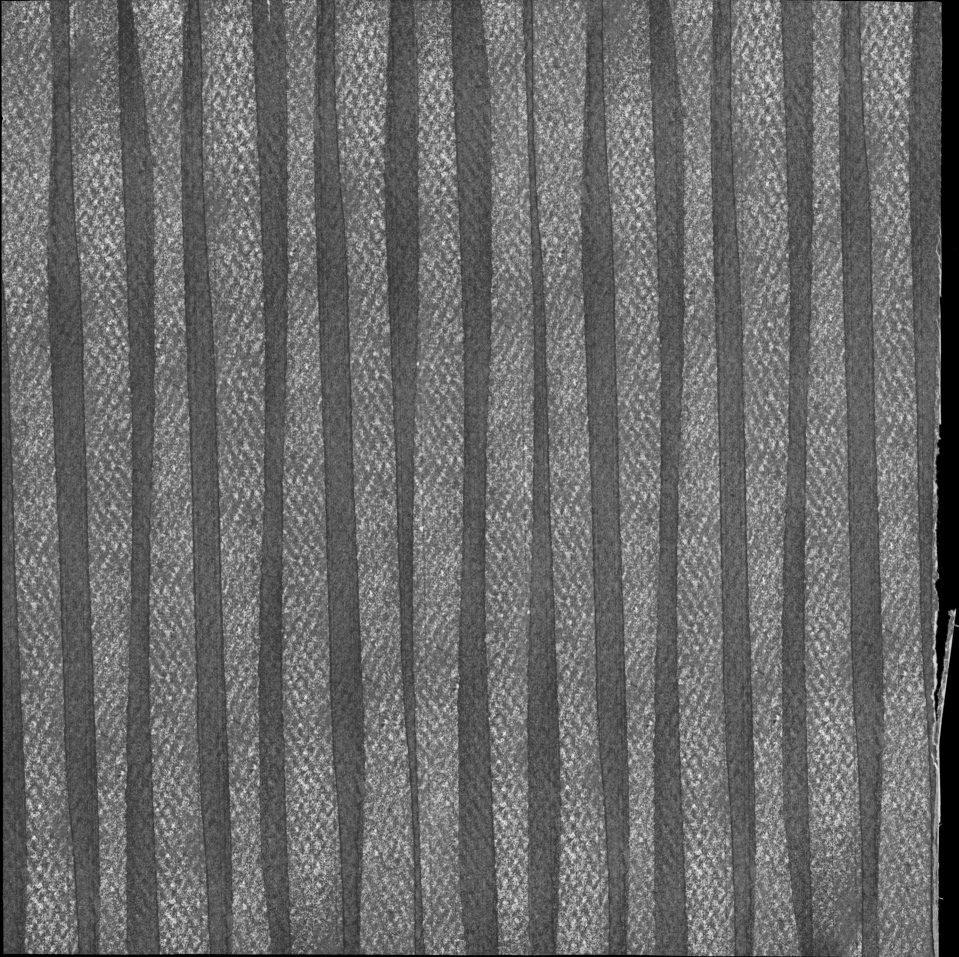

Hot Pink

The Life & Fashions of Elsa Schiaparelli

Susan Goldman Rubin

ABRAMS BOOKS FOR YOUNG READERS · NEW YORK

Library of Congress Cataloging-in-Publication Data
Rubin, Susan Goldman.
Hot pink : the life and fashions of Elsa Schiaparelli / Susan Goldman Rubin.
pages cm
ISBN 978-1-4197-1642-3 (hardcover)
1. Schiaparelli, Elsa, 1890–1973. 2. Fashion design—France—History—20th century—
Juvenile works. 3. Fashion—France—History—20th century—Juvenile works. I. Title.
TT504.6.F7R83 2015
746.9'2—dc23
2014032527

Printed and bound in China
10 9 8 7 6 5 4 3 2

Abrams Books for Young Readers are available at special discounts when
purchased in quantity for premiums and promotions as well as fundraising or
educational use. Special editions can also be created to specification. For details,
contact specialsales@abramsbooks.com or the address below.

THE ART OF BOOKS SINCE 1949

115 West 18th Street
New York, NY 10011

For Olivia Juliet Rubin

Fashion designer Elsa Schiaparelli

(pronounced Skap-a-rell-ee, although she claimed no one ever said it properly) wanted to invent a new color for fashion. A shade never seen before in women's clothes. Something exciting. She thought of the illustrations in her father's books that she had seen as a child and remembered the vivid pink hoods, or *chullos*, worn by the Incas in Peru. She even recalled the bright pink begonias on the terrace that she had admired from her baby carriage. "The color flashed in front of my eyes," she wrote. "Like all the light and the birds and the fish in the world put together. A shocking color."

A shocking-pink taffeta jacket embroidered with jet-bluck beads that Schiap designed and wore in 1947.

Schiap was about six years old when this photograph was taken.

She called it shocking pink, and it became her signature color—the one she would forever be known for. Fashion magazines soon reported that shocking pink was becoming more popular than red. "Schiap," for short, or "Skap," as she was known to everyone, made a shocking-pink collar and leash for her pet dachshund, Nuts, and walked him through the streets of Paris, attracting attention. Her friend, surrealist artist Salvador Dalí, dyed an enormous stuffed polar bear shocking pink to popularize the color, and Schiap put the bear in her boutique.

Just like her artist friends, Schiap delighted the world with her innovations. To her, fashion was art.

rom the start, Schiap caused surprises. When she was born, on September 10, 1890, in Rome, Italy, her parents were expecting a boy. They didn't even have a girl's name picked out. So, at her baptism at St. Peter's Basilica in the Vatican, her nurse named her after herself: Elsa. "Never was a name less appropriate," wrote Schiap. As an adult, she insisted on being called by her nickname.

"Schiap was an ugly child," she wrote about herself in her autobiography. For an Italian girl at that time, she was unfashionably thin and had enormous dark eyes. Her sister, Beatrice, ten years older, was gorgeous. Their mother often made critical remarks about Schiap's looks and told her that she was "as ugly as her sister was beautiful." Schiap believed it and, as a little girl, dreamed up a way to make herself pretty.

If she could make flowers sprout all over her face, she thought, she would be the only woman of her kind in the whole world. So Schiap got some seeds from the gardener and "planted" them in her throat, ears, and mouth. Then she sat waiting for the seeds to bloom. She felt they ought to grow faster in her warm body than in the soil outside, but the result was to make her nearly suffocate. Her mother panicked and sent for the doctor, who removed the seeds. For Schiap, "the chief disappointment was that no flowers grew to turn her into a beauty."

Schiap grew up in the Palazzo (palace) Corsini. Her father, a noted scholar, headed the Lincei Library, located in the palazzo, and the family lived in an elegant apartment there. Surrounded by tapestries and frescoes, Schiap enjoyed art from an early age.

When she was old enough, her father allowed her to look through his rare books. She marveled at the sketches in Leonardo da Vinci's notebooks. When she saw da Vinci's drawing of a "flying machine" and heard about the new sport of parachuting, she decided to try it for herself. Schiap opened a large umbrella, climbed onto the sill of a second-floor window in the palazzo, and "threw herself into space." Luckily, she landed in a soft pile of manure in the garden below. Years later, as a fashion designer, she would create a collection of styles inspired by seeing parachute jumpers on a trip to Russia.

She marveled at the sketches in Leonardo da Vinci's notebooks.

Her uncle Giovanni, a famous astronomer who had discovered canals on Mars, encouraged her curiosity. When the family stayed at his villa near Milan, he helped Schiap look through his telescope at the stars. "He would describe Mars for me as if he had just returned from a long visit [there]," wrote Schiap. She confided in him and bemoaned the moles on her face that she thought made her look plain. Uncle Giovanni pointed out that the spots were actually beauty marks forming the shape of the Big Dipper. "He liked me because he used to say that I was born with the

constellation of the Great Bear [Big Dipper] on my cheek," she wrote.

Fashion interested Schiap from the time she was a little girl. At home in the palazzo, she climbed a ladder into the attic and discovered a trunk filled with her mother's wedding gown and old dresses. "I spent long hours up there, emptying the trunk and trying everything on," she wrote.

On her twelfth birthday, her mother gave her an allowance of fifty lire a month to choose her own clothes. "This was not a great amount even in those days," wrote Schiap, "but I managed to look very well on it. Planning things out on the principle of what we now call 'separates,' I managed to give the impression that I had a lot of clothes." She chose "fine white blouses edged with lace" and wore them with various skirts, an idea she used later in her designs.

School bored her. "The fact that I was obliged to learn things I did not care about and curb my imagination revolted me," she wrote. She rebelled by secretly writing romantic poetry. After a while she gave the poems to her older cousin Attilio to read. He was Uncle Giovanni's son and an art critic. Attilio liked Schiap's poems so much that he showed them to a publisher in Milan, who asked to meet the poet. According to Schiap, she was only fourteen then. Most likely she was fifteen. Pre-

tending she was going on a family visit, she went to Milan, and her cousin took her to the publisher's office. Her poems were published in 1911, when she was twenty-one, and critics quoted excerpts in newspapers throughout Italy.

Schiap's parents, who were very private and traditional, read the poems in manuscript form before they were printed. They were horrified by these poems about love and sorrow and considered the whole thing a disgrace. It was decided that, "as a punishment," Schiap would be sent to a convent in Switzerland.

She quickly grew to hate the strict rules of the convent. She went on a hunger strike, and her father finally came to take her home.

In those days, the early twentieth century, young women raised in a traditional Italian family like Schiap's didn't prepare for a career or trade. Marriage was their only option. But Schiap wasn't interested in any of the men her parents considered a good match for her. Her sister heard from a friend in England, who was looking for someone to help her take care of orphans in a country house. For Schiap, "this was the golden opportunity."

The Big Dipper, which Schiap had adopted as her good-luck charm, was embroidered in silver on a blue velvet jacket for her Zodiac collection in 1938. Her uncle Giovanni had told her that it was good luck to have beauty marks in the shape of the constellation.

She took the job of nanny, and in 1913, at the age of twenty-two, she set out for London, escorted by family friends. Their first stop was Paris.

Upon arriving she announced, "This is the place where I am going to live!"

Paris was the center of the art world. Artists Pablo Picasso and Georges Braque and other cubists were painting in a new, revolutionary style, and Schiap read about them in art magazines. And everywhere she heard talk about the innovative fashions of Paul Poiret.

Poiret had started out by working for Charles Frederick Worth, considered the father of high French fashion, or haute couture. Worth was the first to present his designs on live models so that clients could see how the gowns and outfits would look. Then the customers chose their own fabrics, and their clothing was made to order.

At that time, women wore tight corsets and petticoats beneath their dresses to help shape their figures. Poiret had opened his own fashion house in 1904, when Schiap was fourteen. He'd boasted that he would free women from corsets. Inspired by Japanese kimonos and Middle Eastern caftans, he designed clothing that hung from the shoulders in straight lines instead of accentuating curves.

In 1911, two years before Schiap arrived in Paris, Poiret introduced harem pants (pantaloons), tunics, and turbans for the general public, and the press dubbed this look the "Persian silhouette." Schiap very likely had seen the new style, or at least pictures of it, while she was in Milan.

On Schiap's last night in Paris, she was invited to a ball by one of her father's colleagues. Enthusiastically, Schiap accepted. Since she didn't own an evening dress and had little money, she bought four yards of dark blue crepe de chine (a fine, soft fabric) and two yards of orange silk. Following Poiret's example, Schiap draped the blue material around her body like a tunic and pantaloons, pinned it into place, and used the orange fabric for a sash and a turban.

At the ball she was "a small sensation." However, when she started dancing the tango, the pins began to drop, and her partner quickly danced her out of the room before her gown fell apart. "It was [my] first couturiere's [fashion designer's] failure," she wrote. But she was to bring back the outfit in the 1930s as lounging pajamas.

....

Her partner quickly danced her out of the room before her gown fell apart.

....

OPPOSITE Paul Poiret, 1913.

LEFT Poiret presented these harem pants and tunic as a "fancy dress" costume at a party he threw in 1911.

In England, Schiap was taken to the countryside to begin her job as nanny. But whenever she could, she journeyed to London. One evening she attended a lecture on theosophy, an alternative, mystical form of religious thought. The lecturer was Comte William de Wendt de Kerlor, a handsome young man who was part French, part Swiss, and part Polish. Schiap "listened, spellbound. She even forgot to get up when the audience left," she wrote. A note was delivered to her, asking if she wanted to meet the speaker. She did, and "they talked with what appeared to be a complete communion of ideas," she noted. By morning, they were engaged to be married. When her parents learned of this, they rushed to London and tried to stop the marriage. "But they failed," wrote Schiap. "The wedding took place with no fuss, no white wedding gown—in a registry office" in early 1914.

At first, Schiap was very happy. But she soon found out that her husband was a scoundrel. A phony. He was not a nobleman or a doctor or a professor, as he had claimed. Besides lecturing, he earned money by reading palms and predicting the future. Fortune-telling was against the law in England, and William was sentenced to prison. To escape jail time, he and Schiap fled to France. But World War I had broken out in Europe in August 1914. William was afraid of being drafted, so he decided to go to America, where there might be more opportunities for his schemes.

On the ship crossing the Atlantic, Schiap became friends with Gabrielle Picabia, the wife of "ultra-modern painter" Francis Picabia. Picabia had helped found an anti-art movement called Dada, which questioned what art should be and set out to shock the public. When they arrived in New York City, Gabrielle introduced Schiap to her artist friends, photographers Edward Steichen, Alfred Stieglitz, and Man Ray. Ray was also a surrealist painter who based his images on dreams and imagination.

Meanwhile, Schiap's husband tried to make a living as an author, a psychologist, and a seer. Schiap helped him. A flier promoting his book shows a photo of her gazing into a crystal ball. After five years of marriage, William drifted away and became romantically involved with other women. He left Schiap pregnant and alone. In 1920, she gave birth to a girl and named her Maria Luisa. Schiap "immediately fell in love with her daughter" and nicknamed her Gogo "because of her continual gurgling."

To support herself and the baby, Schiap took odd jobs, such as doing translations for importers. She also received a small allowance from her mother, which she used to pay the nurse who looked after Gogo. When Gogo was fifteen months old, Schiap noticed that the toddler "could hardly walk." She moved "like a crab"—sideways. Schiap took Gogo to a specialist and learned that her child had infantile paralysis—polio. "I reeled under the blow," wrote Schiap. In those days, there was no vaccine for polio. The early, acute stage of infection had left Gogo crippled. Schiap's only thought was: Would her daughter ever walk normally?

A new friend named Blanche Hays offered to help. Blanche was also separated from her husband and had a daughter. The war in Europe had ended in 1918, and Blanche invited Schiap and Gogo to sail to France as her guests and paid for their tickets. Together the young mothers took the children to Paris, where Schiap sought expert medical help for Gogo. Motivated by the need to pay for Gogo's care, Schiap struggled to find ways to make money.

Looking back, she said, "If I have become what I am, I owe it to two distinct things—poverty and Paris. Poverty forced me to work, and Paris gave me a liking for it."

Schiap earned a bit of money by selecting "beautiful things" at auctions and flea markets for antiques dealers to resell in their shops. She also made simple, stylish clothes for herself and her friends Blanche and Gabrielle. Gabrielle was

Noire et Blanche (Black and White), 1926. Man Ray photographed a model beside an African mask, emphasizing the similar oval shapes but the contrasting black and white. He presented imaginative images never seen before, just as Schiap did in her clothing designs.

back in Paris, too, and through her Schiap became part of a circle of artists and poets, including her old friend Man Ray. Ray took her to the artists' favorite cabaret, Le Boeuf sur le Toit (the Ox on the Roof), and introduced her to Pablo Picasso and Jean Cocteau, among others.

Meanwhile, Schiap put Gogo in the care of a French doctor who used an electric treatment to strengthen the child's legs. Gogo lived with the doctor's family in Paris for a few years; then, when she improved, she came back to her mother.

One day, Schiap accompanied a wealthy friend to the salon of Paul Poiret, who was known to say, "Ladies come to me for a gown as they go to a distinguished painter to get their portrait put on canvas. I am an artist, not a dressmaker." He was one of the first to combine art and fashion by commissioning painter Raoul Dufy to design textile patterns. In Poiret's salon, Schiap was excited by what she saw.

"While my friend was choosing dresses, I gazed around, moonstruck," she wrote. Enraptured, she tried things on in front of a full-length mirror. She put on a large velvet coat in vivid stripes and lined with bright blue crepe de chine. "It was magnificent," she said. Suddenly someone said, "Why don't you buy it, mademoiselle? It might have been made for you."

It was Paul Poiret. Schiap said, "I cannot buy it. It is certainly too expensive, and when could I wear it?"

"Don't worry about money," said Poiret, "and *you* could wear anything anywhere." He gave her the coat, then a whole wardrobe of clothes, and invited her to elegant parties at his house. He had opened a design art school for Parisian girls, and he mentored young talent. Although Schiap didn't

attend the school, he admired an evening dress she had made for Gabrielle and encouraged her to think of fashion design as a career.

Schiap had been considering pursuing painting or sculpture, both of which, she noted, she did "fairly well." But she decided to follow Poiret's advice and "invent" dresses and outfits. "Dress designing is to me not a profession but an art," she wrote, echoing Poiret's words. In the 1920s, following World War I, modern women weren't as interested anymore in wearing the lavish garments that Poiret designed. The old, formal lifestyle had changed, and there was a new emphasis on sports and youth.

In response to this trend, fashion designer Gabrielle ("Coco") Chanel introduced comfortable clothing made of jersey, an inexpensive, lightweight fabric used for men's underwear. Inspired by menswear, Chanel produced chic, simple designs in her favorite neutral colors: black, beige, and white. In 1921, she had opened a salon on rue Cambon that was hugely successful. "Women at that time were very sweater minded," wrote Schiap. "Chanel had, for quite a few years, made machine-knitted dresses and jumpers [pullovers]." Chanel also offered turtlenecks and striped tops like the ones worn by sailors and fishermen, as well as wide-legged trousers. With her slim, boyish figure, Chanel was her own best model.

"Dress designing is to me not a profession but an art."

Coco Chanel wearing her "sailor" outfit.

A friend visiting Schiap one afternoon in 1927 happened to be wearing a hand-knitted sweater. It intrigued Schiap, and she asked to meet the person who had made it. She was introduced to an Armenian woman named Aroosiag Mikaelian, known as Mike, who made sweaters in partnership with her brother and a group of knitters they hired. Schiap asked if they could copy a design she would give them. She drew a large "butterfly bow in front, like a scarf 'round the neck." And she said, "The bow must be white against a black [back]ground."

Schiap knew that her design was a "mad idea," but the sister and brother set to work. The first sweater came out lopsided. "The second was better. The third, sensational." The black trompe l'oeil bowknot sweater had a white collar, bow, and cuffs that were actually knitted in but appeared to be attached. Schiap wore the pullover to lunch at a swanky restaurant and "created a furor. All the women wanted one immediately," she wrote. A buyer for Abraham & Straus, a department store in New York, placed an order for forty sweaters with matching skirts that had to be delivered in two weeks. Schiap and the Armenian siblings

hurriedly rounded up more Armenian knitters and finished the job on time.

Schiap had already presented her first small collection of hand-knitted sweaters, jackets, and crepe de chine skirts, which she called "Display No. 1" in January 1927, then another in May. In November of that same year, a wealthy friend sponsored Schiap's fall collection of casual separates, a group of clothes reflecting her unique taste. But her bowknot sweater in the November collection became one of her most copied designs.

The December issue of *Vogue* magazine published a sketch of the trompe l'oeil bowknot sweater and proclaimed it "an artistic masterpiece." The sweater was extremely popular in America and was copied in cheaper versions to be sold at Macy's and Gimbels department stores. The November 1928 issue of *Ladies' Home Journal* even published instructions for knitting the "chic bowknot sweater." Inspired and filled with confidence, Schiap "became very daring," she said, and added wild designs for her knits: "pierced hearts

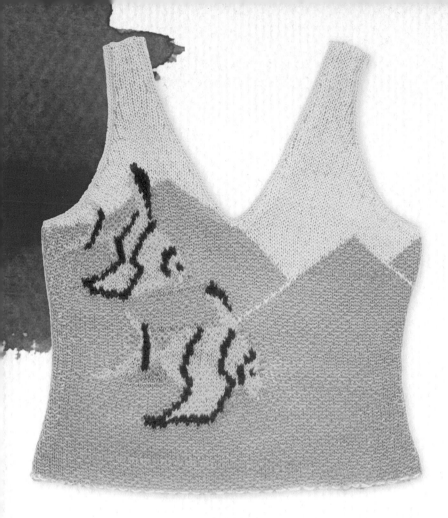

shopping street. Four, she said, was her lucky number. Now she had a salesroom, workroom, living room, and bedroom, all in one place. Framed pictures of Gogo were displayed on the mantel. A black-and-white sign on the front door downstairs announced SCHIAPARELLI, and beneath it, *POUR LE SPORT*.

She specialized in sport clothes. Schiap showed one- and two-piece knitted bathing suits in stripes and with a pattern of "fish wriggling on the stomach." She invented wraparound dresses and skirts that tied like aprons to wear at the beach, and lounging pajamas that could go over a bathing suit. She made golf suits and skiwear with matching gloves and hoods that were shaped like the Peruvian *chullos* she had admired in her father's books.

American aviator Charles Lindbergh's flight across the Atlantic Ocean inspired people to go up in the first modern passenger planes. So Schiap designed one-piece flying suits for women that were like overalls. Upon arriving at a destination, a woman could whisk the suit off and be smartly dressed underneath. She became acquainted with pioneer pilot Amelia Earhart and made linen overalls especially for her. New York department stores such as Saks Fifth Avenue and Best & Co. sold Schiap's originals and also made copies.

and snakes," like a sailor's tattoos, and "a skeleton sweater" that made headlines.

Schiap partnered with businessman Charles Kahn, who was connected with a leading Paris department store, Galeries Lafayette. She had been turning out clothes in her little apartment at 20 rue de l'Université and displaying them on tables. But her customers had no place to sit down. With her growing success, she needed more space, and in 1928 she moved to a garret (a small attic) at 4 rue de la Paix, a fashionable

In 1928, Schiap sent Gogo, now eight years old, to a boarding school in Lausanne, Switzerland, to be near a leading specialist in polio. Although Schiap wanted her daughter to receive the best possible care, it broke her heart to have her so far away. "It was our first real, serious separation," wrote Schiap, "and I was deeply affected at having to leave her so young."

In November 1929, she took a trip to New York City to oversee her latest collection at Stewart & Company, another department store on Fifth Avenue that later became Bonwit Teller. An American silk manufacturer invited her to create a collection of beach pajamas for resort wear using its vivid staccato prints. An ad described the pajamas as portraying "the zing and abruptness of modern life."

Twice a year, Schiap presented her collection for the following season. "For those who do not know it, a winter collection is made in the sweltering heat," she wrote. "The summer collection is made in the dark of the winter, with an electric light and the nearly naked girls shivering in their bathing suits."

Schiap's sportswear was followed by her first evening dress, a simple black gown with a short, cropped white jacket she called a bolero. She presented it in May 1930 for her fall collection.

"This proved [to be] the most successful dress of my career," she wrote. "It was reproduced all over the world." Her friend Man Ray took stunning pictures of Schiap modeling everything from the gown to silk pajamas for major fashion magazines. He seldom photographed the side of her face with the moles; if he did, he softened his camera's focus or retouched the pictures in his darkroom.

Another shot, taken later by photojournalist John Phillips for *Life* magazine, shows Schiap smiling, in profile, with the beauty marks on her cheek clearly visible. She's smartly put together in a jacket and hat of her own design, and she's wearing her favorite bracelet, a jeweled snake coiled around her wrist. Schiap compensated for what she believed to be her lack of naturally pretty features with her great style and helped other women do the same. She took pride in transforming women like herself (and even movie actresses) into extraordinary creatures "who stirred interest and curiosity" by wearing her clothes and accessories. "I tried to help them find their type," she wrote. "This I believe to be the secret of being well dressed." Photographs of her designs in leading fashion magazines set the standards of beauty for those times.

This photo of Schiap by John Phillips shows the beauty marks on her face that her uncle Giovanni said resembled the pattern of the Big Dipper constellation.

When Schiap first started out, she knew nothing about dressmaking. But she formed principles based on the artwork that had surrounded her in childhood in the palazzo. For her, clothes had to be architectural. "The body . . . must be used as a frame is used in a building," she said. She draped and cut fabric directly on the models, the way Poiret had done. Sometimes, though, she did draw sketches first. She then teamed up with the finest embroiderers in Paris to execute her designs.

Orders piled in for her creations, and she hired three young women to assist her. Together they were "like the leaves of a four-leaf clover," she wrote. Schiap believed that the way for someone to learn about fashion design was to start at the lowest level, "as an *arpette*, the girl who picks the pins from the floor." She said, "The best and only school is the workroom, noisy, human, alive, and creative."

Her business grew incredibly fast, and the attic became too small to hold the crush of clients. So she moved downstairs to better, larger rooms and hired more and more people to produce her designs. Soon she took over the whole second floor of her building. She had an interior designer arrange the salon to look like a boat. Scarves, sweaters, and belts hung from ropes on the white walls, and black wooden armchairs resembled those on the deck of a ship.

Schiap regularly took time off to visit her daughter, who was now nearly nine, and found Gogo improving. "She had even learned to ski and to ride [horses]," wrote Schiap. "The doctors were delighted."

She took pride in transforming women like herself into extraordinary creatures.

Just as her business was thriving, Schiap received an emergency phone call from Lausanne. Gogo needed an operation immediately for a burst appendix. Schiap gave the doctors her permission over the phone, then hopped onto a train to Switzerland to be with her daughter. But after the surgery, Gogo suffered from a severe infection. "She was between life and death for a month," wrote Schiap.

When this happened, Schiap was in the mid-dle of designing what she called her first "real collection" for her new salon. It had to be ready on schedule. "It was practically made in the train," wrote Schiap. "I would travel at night, stay a day and night in Lausanne, and return to Paris for two days' work . . . I never knew if I was going to find Gogo smiling or limp. I never dared to hope."

"At last she got better," wrote Schiap, "and I had my first real show" in January 1929. Models paraded the clothes before an audience. "It was, of course, a very important event and vastly successful," she wrote. The *Paris Times* in February 1929 reviewed the show and called Elsa "one of the rare creators." The simplicity of her clothes particularly appealed to American women, and department stores snapped them up. Manufacturers copied the designs and mass-produced them. Schiap didn't care, because the clothes handmade by her staff in rich materials looked entirely different from the machine-made copies. "All the laws about protection from copyists are vain and useless," she wrote. "The moment that people stop copying you, it means that you are no longer any good and that you have ceased to be news." The *Ladies' Home Journal* published Schiap's patterns so that skillful women could sew the clothes themselves. American movie actresses became her clients, both on screen and off. Women in the theater audience wanted to look like the glamorous stars and imitated their outfits.

Around 1930, Schiap came up with a design for a little knitted cap like a tube that fit snugly and could be shaped however one liked. Movie stars Katharine Hepburn and Ina Claire wore the cap, and it became wildly popular. An American manufacturer bought one of them and started his own multimillion-dollar business producing "Mad Caps." They were sold everywhere. Schiap said she "got so tired of seeing it reproduced that she wished she had never thought of it," and she ordered her salesgirls to destroy every cap in stock and never mention it again.

At this time the Great Depression had hit both sides of the Atlantic. The stock market had crashed in 1929. Banks failed around the world, and millions of people were out of work. Many of the big fashion houses in Paris went bankrupt and closed. Even the popular designer Chanel, now Schiap's rival, suffered a decline in business. But Schiap's business continued to grow. She worked with American manufacturers and used their fabrics to bring out a line of affordable outfits. She made aprons and kitchen clothes so that American women who no longer had servants "could do their own cooking and still look attractive." In Paris, she stopped using expensive silk and adapted French

A young woman in the 1920s sports a ladylike pleated skirt and jacket trimmed in dainty lace. This is very different from Schiap's unique bowknot sweater, where the "blouse and bow" are knitted into one playful pullover.

synthetics, such as rayon, to lower costs. Her rich, private clients stayed with her and, despite the hard times, demanded more of her innovative designs.

By 1932, Schiap had a staff of four hundred employees turning out thousands of garments in eight ateliers (workshops where a master designer and assistants produced pieces). There were tailors, fitters, cutters, junior designers, sewing girls, *arpettes*, mannequins (models), and saleswomen.

Mike, the Armenian knitter who had made the bowknot sweater, had a workroom of her own. "All this in five years from scratch," commented American journalist Janet Flanner in the *New Yorker* magazine in June 1932. The piece described Schiap's "comet-like rise" in the fashion world. "She is ranked even by her detractors as leader of The Young School in Paris dressmaking," wrote Flanner. Chanel spitefully referred to her as "that Italian who's making clothes." Some of Chanel's best customers switched to Schiap because they loved her originality and wit.

Schiap's business had expanded so rapidly that "the walls seemed to groan under the impact of growing crowds," she said. Once again she needed to move to a bigger place. Her mentor, Poiret, offered his house on Paris's most famous and stylish street, the Champs-Élysées. But Schiap wanted to stay in her district, which was noted for high fashion. In 1935 she opened the House of Schiaparelli, at 21 Place Vendôme, "the world's center of elegance."

"Here is undoubtedly the greatest cluster of wealth in Paris," she wrote. Her salon was surrounded by banks, jewelers, and luxurious hotels, such as the Ritz.

Schiap now lived in an apartment nearby and walked to work when the weather was good. The interior designer who had created the boat motif for her on the rue de la Paix decorated her new home in a stark, modern style with white rubber material for the curtains and chairs, and the same material in bright green for the sofas. The black dining tables featured black dinnerware. When Schiap gave her first dinner party there, she invited Chanel. "At the sight of this modern furniture and black plates, she [Chanel] shuddered as if she were passing a cemetery," recalled Schiap with glee.

She showed her first Place Vendôme collection in February 1935. It was called Stop, Look, and Listen. Through fashion, Schiap wanted to make people take notice of other countries and cultures. She had observed a fourteen-year-old Indian princess visiting Paris wearing exquisite saris. So she designed a slender gown like a sari that wrapped around the body and could be worn with scarves called *ihrams*.

Another idea came from a visit to a fish market in Copenhagen, Denmark. The old women selling the fish "wore on their heads newspapers twisted into queer shapes of hats," wrote Schiap. Back in Paris, she contacted a textile manufacturer and said, "I want a material printed like a newspaper."

"It will never sell!" he replied.

"I think it will," said Schiap.

Schiap clipped newspaper articles about her-

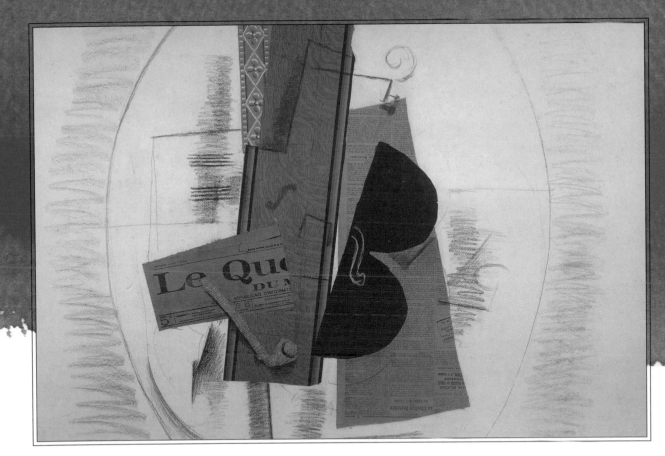

self, even those that were not complimentary, and pieced them together like a puzzle. Then she had them printed on silk and cotton. Her decision to assemble the clippings like a collage was inspired by Picasso's and Braque's cubist still lifes that included scraps of newspaper. Schiap's fabric came in various colors, and she used it to make blouses, scarves, handbags, men's neckties, and beach hats. The fabric sold well for twenty years.

"I had always loved materials," wrote Schiap, "and I worked more closely with the textile people than did any of my colleagues." She launched novelty fabrics made of cellophane, straw, and glass.

She became excited about tweeds and tartans and visited factories in England and Scotland where they were produced. While in Great Britain, she thrilled at seeing black sheep for the first time. "I had them shorn," she wrote, "and the wool was made up for me in the most startling materials."

Schiap had opened a branch of her business in London in 1933, with workrooms above the salon. "My staff was courteous and capable," she wrote. However, she argued with her English staff about their traditionally British tea break. Schiap was known for her strict work habits, and punctuality was key. "Always on time, five minutes early," was her motto. She came to the office precisely at ten o'clock every morning and was furious if any of her staff arrived even one minute late. It was said she worked harder than anyone else till seven in the evening.

Within her salon at Place Vendôme, Schiap opened a separate boutique on the ground floor. It was "the very first of its kind," she boasted, "and has since been copied all over the world." Her unique idea was to sell skirts, blouses, sweaters, lingerie, handbags, shoes, scarves, and fun jewelry made of glass and wood right "off the rack." "It became instantaneously famous because of the formula of 'ready to be taken away immediately,'" she wrote. Even her regular clients, who had clothes made to order at the salon, enjoyed shopping in the boutique. Other top fashion designers scorned the idea. But the boutique became "one of the sights of Paris. Tourists came to photograph it," said Schiap. "The boutique took its rightful place as a Paris landmark."

Inside the boutique was a floor-to-ceiling gilded birdcage displaying perfumes. Schiap, like other fashion designers, developed and sold her own line of fragrances. Poiret had been the first to establish a perfume and cosmetics company in 1911, which he named after his eldest daughter, Rosine. Chanel had brought out a perfume in 1921 called Chanel N°5 that was an immediate hit. Packaged in a plain, square bottle, it is still a worldwide best seller.

Schiap wanted each of her perfumes to start with the initial of her last name. The first, in 1928, was simply called S. But the most successful perfume, introduced in 1937, was named Shocking, after her signature color, shocking pink.

Shocking pink came about as Elsa tried to invent a new shade with the help of Jean Clément, an artist, jeweler, and chemist who baked buttons for her unique clothing. Together, they kept experimenting. Jean tried working with a varnish normally used for custom-built cars. With an airbrush he sprayed drops of the varnish onto white paper. First, he mixed a pink the color of a typical cameo. No. Then a dusty rose. No. Then, one day in 1937, Jean added a streak of magenta to the pink. That was it! Schiap named it "shocking pink," and it became her trademark. She designed an entire collection of gowns, jackets, and caps in shocking pink. "It caused a mild panic among my friends," she said. They thought she was crazy. No one would buy clothes in that color, they said. But people did. Shocking pink "set the fashion world spinning."

A magazine advertisement for Shocking perfume, talc, and lipstick.

"The success was immense and immediate," wrote Schiap. The September 1937 issue of *Vogue* magazine featured a shocking-pink gown and was a sensation. *Harper's Bazaar* magazine for October 1937 did a whole page on shocking-pink accessories. Schiap loved the color and was sure that others would, too. "Dare to be different" was her motto. Later, in the 1950s, shocking pink was called hot pink.

The bottle that held Shocking perfume was shaped like the curvaceous body of actress Mae West. West was famous for her full, voluptuous figure. At one point she needed costumes for a new movie and also a wardrobe for herself, but she couldn't travel from Hollywood to Paris for fittings. So she had a plaster dress form made of her hourglass figure and sent it to Paris instead. When Schiap introduced her perfume Shocking,

Schiap loved to ski and took Gogo, age fourteen, to St. Moritz, Switzerland, in 1934.

first designer to truly "brand" herself. Chanel used her name for perfume only, but Schiap leased her name to girdles, watches, nail polish, paper dolls, sunglasses, jewelry, shoes, swimsuits, and handbags.

"We worked hard," she wrote, "but we had fun. The collections followed one another with definite themes."

Schiap was the first designer to truly "brand" herself.

Meanwhile, Gogo, now fourteen, had left the boarding school in Switzerland. Schiap decided to send her to Abbot's Hill School for girls in Hertfordshire, England. Gogo turned out to be a good athlete and particularly loved English outdoor sports. Schiap visited her daughter as often as she could. In the summer and winter, they took vacations together. But once, a whole term went by when Schiap was too busy in Paris to come see Gogo at school. So they met in London for a weekend, and Schiap was "stupefied by the sight of her." Gogo stood there "in a horrible blue uniform." She had put on too much weight eating starchy school food. From then on, Schiap said, "I

she adapted West's torso for the design of the bottle and topped it with a tiny bouquet of colorful glass flowers. By using her own name on everything from perfumes to scarves, Schiap was the went as often as I could on Sundays to release Gogo from potatoes and pudding." Gogo usually invited a couple of friends to join them for lunch. "As we drove away from the school," wrote Schiap, "we would invariably meet several other girls waiting behind the bushes to be picked up." Together, they all feasted at a village restaurant.

In 1937, Schiap bought an eighteen-room mansion at 22 rue de Berri. "I saw it, loved it, and felt I belonged to it," she wrote. "The number in the street was also my lucky number: 22, two plus two equals four." The old mansion was "a little shabby," but it had a "deep green garden hiding in the middle of Paris." The house was not meant as a salon to show her collections but as a personal retreat. Schiap filled it with treasures gathered during her travels or on drives through the countryside. Her favorite room was the library, where she spent evenings surrounded by "beloved paintings put anywhere, on the floor, on chairs, against ancient Chinese bronzes," and "books, books, books."

Around this time she began collaborating with her friends Salvador Dalí and Jean Cocteau. They were part of the surrealist movement, basing their art on dreams and fantasies. Schiap, with her "fan-tastic imagination" and "daredevil approach," was not only accepted in the surrealist circle, but she also influenced their work.

"Schiaparelli is, above all, a dressmaker of eccentricity," wrote Cocteau in *Harper's Bazaar* for April 1937. "Her establishment in Place Vendôme is a devil's laboratory."

Schiap had a passion for zippers, which she called zips, and she used them decoratively before any other fashion designer did. In the late 1920s and early 1930s, metal zippers mainly fastened galoshes, men's tobacco pouches and trousers, and children's clothes. Schiap had plastic "zips" dyed special colors to contrast with the fabric of her outfits. "Not only did they appear for the first time," she wrote, "but in the most unexpected places, even on evening clothes."

"Why don't you zip yourself into your evening dresses?" wrote Diana Vreeland in her "Why Don't You" column in *Harper's Bazaar* in March 1936.

"Artists took much more part in the life and development of fashion than they do now," Schiap wrote in 1954. Working with Dalí, Cocteau, and Man Ray gave Schiap a "sense of exhilaration." She felt "supported and understood."

"Dalí was a constant caller," she wrote. "We devised together the coat with many drawers from one of his famous pictures." The painting, titled

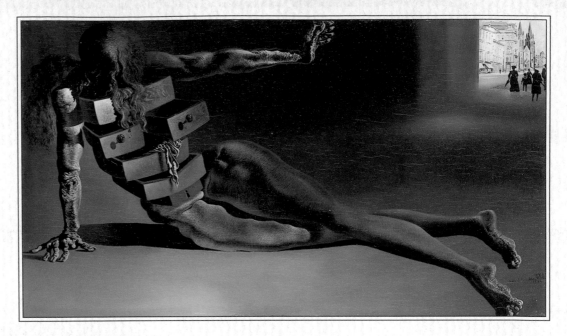

The Anthropomorphic Cabinet, features drawers opening from the torso of a naked man sitting on the floor. The drawers hold secrets, which spill out in dreams or psychiatric sessions. Dalí made a sketch for a garment that looked just like a chest of drawers, and Schiap produced suits and coats from the drawing. The "desk suit" jacket had five "drawer" pockets with black plastic handles. Some of the drawers were real; others were fake. Yet the outfit was considered very wearable and chic. Photographer Cecil Beaton took pictures of women modeling the suits in a surrealistic setting.

Another motif of Dalí's was the lobster. He began by painting a portrait of his beloved wife, Gala, with a lobster on her head. Then he made a mixed-media *Lobster Telephone*. With Schiap he designed a lobster dress. Dalí placed an orangey-red lobster amid sprigs of parsley on the skirt of a white organdy gown. The fabric was printed by a superb silk manufacturer. The story goes that Dalí wanted to spread mayonnaise on the finished lobster gown, but Schiap objected. The gown became famous when Beaton photographed it for *Vogue* magazine.

Schiap and Dalí attracted more publicity with their design for a black hat in the form of a shoe with a shocking-pink heel. The idea sprang from a photograph of Dalí jokingly wearing his wife's high-heeled pump upside down on his head. One of Schiap's most well-dressed, elegant clients "had the courage to wear it," wrote Schiap appreciatively. Dalí liked taking ordinary things and using them in a "mad" new way. He said it was "fantasy combined with a certain sense of fashion."

The next Schiap-Dalí innovation was a hat resembling a lamb chop. Dalí had painted a picture of himself at age eight with a raw chop on his head. Schiap wore this number "defiantly" and said that it contributed most of all to her "fame for eccentricity."

With Jean Cocteau, a filmmaker as well as a graphic artist and novelist, she collaborated on evening clothes. Cocteau made line drawings of two women's heads, and Schiap had them embroidered on the back of a long jersey coat.

This woman in an elegant gown typical of the 1930s is ready for a night on the town. However, the dress lacks the imaginative designs that Schiap dreamed up for evening wear with Jean Cocteau and other great artists of the time.

The heads in profile, with pursed red lips, faced each other and were topped by a bouquet of pink silk roses. But the image could be viewed another way, too. The space between the heads could appear to be an urn holding flowers, the urn resting on a column formed by lines of parallel stitches going down the back of the coat. This kind of ambiguous image was a common theme of the surrealists.

OPPOSITE Evening coat designed by Schiap and Jean Cocteau, 1937.

RIGHT Black gloves with red snakeskin fingernails designed by Schiap, 1936–37.

BELOW A film still from *Beauty and the Beast* by Jean Cocteau, 1946.

Hands were another usual subject. Man Ray photographed a model's hands that Picasso had painted to look like gloves. Schiap designed black suede gloves with red snakeskin "fingernails" to look like hands. The photos and the gloves raised a typical question of surrealism: what is real, and what isn't?

Cocteau explored the theme further in his film *Beauty and the Beast*, a retelling of the fairy tale. At the end of the film, of course, the Beast is transformed into a prince. The change from ugly to beautiful was a popular theme for the surrealists and for Schiap, too.

She took their symbol of transformation, the butterfly, and used it for her summer collection of 1937. Schiap designed a fabric printed with colorful butterflies fluttering against a pink background and made it into a gorgeous dress that was a best seller in America. She trimmed straw hats with big butterfly pins and bunches of flowers. And life-size butterfly buttons adorned a suit jacket.

Diana Vreeland dedicated her February 1937 column in *Harper's Bazaar* to the inspiration of Schiaparelli. Diana had lived in Europe for a few years and dressed stylishly. So in her column, she passed on ideas from high society to middle-class American women. Addressing her readers, she wrote, "Why don't you realize that this wonderfully creative woman is expressing our life and times in her little suits and dresses and unique materials?"

"Not one looked like what a button was supposed to look like."

uttons, for Schiap, were an art form all their own. She detested ordinary round ones and never used them. Jean Clément, who had helped develop the color shocking pink, produced her button designs, baking them in a small electric oven. "He was a genius," she wrote, "a real French artisan who would work with such burning love that he was almost a fanatic." The buttons were made of all

kinds of materials: china, plastic, colored crystal, sealing wax, amber, and hand-carved wood. There were buttons in the shapes of spoons, snails, padlocks, fishhooks, paper clips, lollipops, bells, and tiny hands holding flowers that were replicas of Victorian brooches, and one set consisted of small hand mirrors. "Not one looked like what a button was supposed to look like," wrote Schiap with pride. Naturally, their shapes related to the theme of every collection. And themed collections were another of her "firsts." Each one showcased a fresh palette of colors, as with the launch of her most famous color, shocking pink, in spring 1937.

For Schiap's Circus collection, presented in February 1938, Clément made cast-metal buttons in the form of flying acrobats to fasten a pink jacket embroidered with dancing horses. More acrobats swung from trapezes on a necklace. There were buttons shaped like peppermint sticks, cotton candy, and clowns. Handbags looked like balloons. Hats resembled ice-cream cones. The Circus collection was one of Schiap's greatest triumphs—"the most riotous and swaggering collection," she wrote.

And the presentation really was a circus. Live acrobats jumped in and out of the salon's windows from ladders propped against the outer wall.

Inside, performers skipped up and down the grand staircase and leaped onto and off the salesgirls' desks.

Celebrities, movie stars, artists, and royalty, as well as dress buyers, crowded the rooms to see the show. "The mannequins [models] had to fight their way through the salons," recalled one fashion editor. "It was just marvelous," said Ragna Fischer, a Danish fashion journalist. "I remember especially the colors, the hysteria and tension."

Whereas other designers presented their new clothes with a sedate parade of models, Schiap originated the concept of a fashion runway show as entertainment, with dramatic lighting and music. She gave four of these presentations a year. Patrons and the press clamored for the best seats. Chanel would remain hidden during a showing of her own latest fashions, but Schiap was always conspicuous at hers. She stood in a doorway near the stairs, observing the reaction of her audience.

One of her clients, Lady Charles Mendl, a famed interior designer, held a circus ball that summer. Schiap attended wearing another innovative design: evening sandals with cork platform soles. These were the first "wedgies," and Schiap

Butterfly dress, 1937.

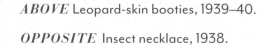

ABOVE Leopard-skin booties, 1939–40.

OPPOSITE Insect necklace, 1938.

danced in them till five o'clock in the morning. She had designed them with shoemaker André Perugia, who collaborated with her on many footwear novelties: high-heeled, buttoned booties in striped leather and silk; boots fringed with monkey fur cascading to the floor; and leopard-skin booties that Schiap wore for bowling.

With Jean Clément she introduced the first shoulder bag. She had asked Clément to adapt the small pouch worn by French railway guards that hung at the end of a strap. Schiap then lengthened the strap, enlarged the bag to be like the ones bus conductors wore to collect fares, and called it the *bandoulière*, or shoulder-strap bag. It became the rage in Paris, and everybody wondered what Schiap would do next.

eanwhile, "Gogo was going places," wrote Schiap. Gogo left Abbot's Hill School in England and went to a school in Paris for a year. When Gogo was sixteen, in 1936, Schiap was asked to write an open letter to her daughter about fashion for the *Daily Express*, a British newspaper.

She began, "Dear Gogo, Soon now you will be

buying your own clothes, so . . . I suppose I ought to give you a little advice.

"To begin with, you won't have a big dress allowance, because I think it is a bad thing for young people . . . Your first inclination will surely be to buy as much as you can for your money. Don't give in to it . . ."

Schiap believed that it was better to have a few well-tailored clothes that fit properly than many cheap, trendy outfits.

Two years later, Schiap opened a debutante department in her London salon, with clothes for young women her daughter's age. By then Gogo was eighteen, but Schiap didn't want her daughter to be involved in her haute couture business. And Gogo willingly stayed away from the world of fashion. She had gone from Paris to Munich to learn German but wound up taking cooking lessons. Gogo returned to London and "lived an enchanting life of early theatres, dance suppers, impressive balls," wrote Schiap, and "for the first time enjoyed beautiful clothes."

In April 1938, Schiap presented a Pagan collection that included her insect necklace. Lifelike insects made by a Tiffany jeweler inside a transparent plastic collar made it appear as if the bugs were crawling on the wearer's skin. Later that year came Schiap's Zodiac collection, inspired by her memories of gazing at the stars with her astronomer uncle. This was one of Schiap's last big collections. War was threatening to erupt again in Europe.

Yet Schiap carried on. In the fall, she brought out her line for spring 1939. The theme was Modern Comedy, a reimagining of costumes from sixteenth-century Italian theater.

Although these were hard times, there were still big parties to attend. Lady Mendl hosted a formal event at the British Embassy, and Gogo wore an evening dress from her mother's Music collection, which had been presented in April 1939. The gown featured musical notes and bars embroidered in red, blue, and gold. The belt buckle was an actual music box that played a melody.

Gogo's clothes always made the news, so Schiap decided to design a line of Junior Miss fashions. They were manufactured by an American firm and sold through Bonwit Teller, a department store on New York's Fifth Avenue.

In the summer of 1939, Schiap closed her London salon because "of the immense problems of a world on the eve of war." In Paris, she dressed her window in Place Vendôme with a peace theme: "a big world globe with flying white doves and one bird sitting upon it with an olive branch in its beak." It was, she said, "a pathetic effort to help a lost cause. Then came September and the declaration of war."

Germany bombed Poland on September 1, 1939, and two days later France and Great Britain declared war on Germany. This was the beginning of World War II. The French government requested that all businesses remain open.

Schiap's staff was reduced from six hundred employees to one hundred and fifty. "The little black school desks where my salesgirls sat near the entrance were half empty!" she wrote. "The men were gone. We had no tailors." But she and other French fashion designers realized the importance of maintaining the dressmaking industry—as a source of income for her remaining workers and for the nation's morale. The House of Schiaparelli stayed open. Chanel, however, stopped production.

Schiap prepared a new Cash and Carry collection. Jackets featured huge pockets so that a woman who "had to leave home in a hurry, or to go on duty without a bag, could pack all that was necessary to her." The collection included one-piece suits that zipped up the front and had zippered pockets designed to hold flashlights, identification papers, and, of course, shocking-pink lipstick.

Schiap's mansion on rue de Berri was next door to the Belgian Embassy. A secret passage connected the two buildings. Refugees "poured in to seek advice and shelter," she wrote. Schiap helped by serving hot coffee and bread. "The bar in my cellar became a well-known meeting place for British officers who were steadily arriving," she wrote, "and for American ambulance drivers who had volunteered, and for women of the French

Mechanized Transport Corps." Gogo joined the corps and "was soon driving a six-wheeled truck," wrote Schiap.

Meanwhile Schiap and her reduced staff did the best they could to produce clothes. Tweed skirts were split for bicycling, which had become the main form of transportation, since gas was rationed and unavailable. Because of the lack of materials for buttons, she used dog chains to fasten jackets and skirts. The words of the latest song about wartime restrictions were printed on a scarf: "Monday—no meat, Wednesday—no butter, but Sunday—*toujours l'amour* [always love]."

She and other French fashion designers realized the importance of maintaining the dressmaking industry— as a source of income for her remaining workers and for the nation's morale.

When Schiap was not at Place Vendôme, she worked with the Salvation Army, "visiting their wonderful canteens and rest houses near the front." The Salvation Army commissioner asked her to design a modern dress for the women workers, like the one she wore. The new uniform was blue with a red collar and blue apron, "but we did not have time to put it into production," she wrote.

The war in Europe escalated as German troops advanced toward France.

"The Americans were recalled to their country on whatever transport they could find," wrote Schiap, "and I convinced the unwilling Gogo that, as an American citizen, she should leave." Gogo had come to France from the United States when she was six. Her nationality could have been Polish or French like her father's, Italian like her mother's, or American, since she was born in New York. Schiap had left the decision up to her daughter. "She chose to be American," she wrote.

Now Schiap insisted that Gogo leave for America immediately. Escorted by a chaperone, she caught the last boat from Genoa and reached New York on June 10, 1940. "On the ship Gogo met her destiny in the form of a handsome young American," wrote Schiap. His name was Robert "Berry" Berenson, and he was a representative in Europe for the shipping company Grace Line.

This article in the *Kingston Daily Freeman*, in Kingston, New York, announces Schiap's arrival in America and her upcoming "Clothes and the Woman" lecture tour.

Gogo had left Paris just in time. "A black cloud enveloped the city," wrote Schiap. On June 14, German troops marched into Paris, and the French surrendered. Schiap heard the news over the radio at a meeting of fashion designers and their representatives. "My work-people, standing white-faced and taut . . . burst into tears," she wrote.

Schiap was determined to do everything she could "for the country of her adoption." She had signed a contract to give lectures on "Clothes and the Woman" in America, and her colleagues urged her to go. Perhaps she could persuade the Americans to come to the aid of France. "I was not an emissary of politics," she wrote, "but a woman engaged in a great craft."

When she crossed the border between France and Spain en route to the United States, the customs officer stamped her visa and said, "Will you make a dress for my wife when you come back?"

Schiap arrived in New York on July 20, 1940. Gogo and Robert, "a huge young man beaming shyly," were waiting for her. Also waiting for her was her partner in her perfume company and her publicity manager.

On her American tour, Schiap was warmly welcomed. "American hospitality is wonderful because it is sincere and exhilarating," she wrote. Wearing her new "Rocket Red" coat, she visited forty-two cities in eight weeks. In Oklahoma City, a Native American chief and his daughter took her around in a streamlined car decorated with enormous shocking-pink bows. In Dallas, Texas, she became the first European designer to win a fashion award. At each stop, Schiap was mobbed by huge crowds.

She told Americans about the troubles in France and the tragedy of its defeat. She said how important it was for France to be saved and, among so many other achievements, continue its "particular creative work," fashion design. Profits from the tour were distributed by the Quakers to children in unoccupied zones of southern France.

Back in New York City, Schiap announced that she had to return to Paris to check on her business. She had appointed an assistant designer to run the salon and workrooms in her absence. Gogo begged Schiap to stay. She and Robert were now engaged. "But in spite of my love of her and tremendously deep emotional tie," wrote Schiap, "I could not hold back." On January 4, 1941, Schiap sailed away, "leaving my little Gogo in tears but in the arms of a strong and reliable American young man."

Woman's dinner jacket, featuring carrot and cauliflower buttons, 1941.

When Schiap left, she was wearing one of her best hats. "It was no ordinary hat," she wrote, "for into the fur trimming I had sewn several thousand dollars that American friends had given me to take to old friends who had been left destitute in France." As she tried to make her way back to Paris, she hurriedly caught a train from Vichy and accidentally left her hat behind. Schiap was frantic but had to go on with her journey. When she finally arrived at rue de Berri, she found her house in good order, and at Place Vendôme, work continued. "I was still worrying about my lost hat," she wrote, "when a woman I knew came to see me wearing it. She had rescued it in Vichy and hoped I would not mind if she kept it because she loved it. I tore it off her head, ran into my room, dug out the money intact from the fur, and gave the hat back to her with joy. And so the friends of my friends got something to eat."

By May, the American foreign minister urged Schiap to leave France with him. "The minister knew I was foolishly in real danger," she wrote. Food and fuel were scarce, and Parisians starved as the Germans took first pick of supplies. "My own situation was uneasy and becoming more and more difficult," wrote Schiap. Although she had become a French citizen, the Germans considered her an Italian. She had family in Italy, and her daughter was an American. "I found myself rather on the spot," wrote Schiap.

Before leaving France, she designed a summer collection celebrating the simple life of the French countryside. A wool and velvet jacket was embroidered with fruits and vegetables from a typical French kitchen garden, and the buttons were shaped like miniature cauliflowers and carrots. Reluctantly, Schiap entrusted her business to longtime associates: her director, her secretary, and her assistant designer. She turned her mansion on rue de Berri over to the Brazilian minister, and on May 11, 1941, she left Paris.

"The minister knew I was foolishly in real danger."

In New York City, she was again greeted by Gogo and Robert, her new son-in-law. The couple had married in March. Now, upon her return to America, Schiap received many offers to start new dressmaking ventures, but she turned them down out of loyalty to Place Vendôme. She didn't want to compete with her business in Paris and other French fashion houses.

Instead, she did relief work and organized exhibitions of French culture to raise money for France. She helped arrange a series of concerts performed by the celebrated French pianist and composer Robert Casadesus with his wife, Gaby, playing the flute. Her old friend Marcel Duchamp, a Dada artist "who had startled the world with his famous painting of a naked woman descending a staircase," was also in New York. They had been introduced many years ago by Man Ray on Schiap's first visit to the city. Duchamp collaborated with her to put on an exhibition of eighty paintings by various artists such as Pablo Picasso, Salvador Dalí, Fernand Léger, and Moïse Kisling. Some works by Picasso had never been seen before in America, and the show was a huge success. Schiap also raised funds for the Quakers to provide bread for children in France.

At age fifty-one, Schiap went to school at the American Red Cross to become a nurse's aide. "All this was new to me," she wrote. She learned how to take temperatures, treat burns, and stop bleeding from wounds. The work "filled her with passionate interest," she wrote, "and gave her a feeling of self-respect."

Then, on December 7, 1941, the Japanese bombed Pearl Harbor in Hawaii, and the United States entered the war. Schiap cheered America's "unanimous and immediate call for action." Her son-in-law left the Grace Line shipping company and enlisted in the army. He was sent to Italy and was awarded a commission while in action. Later he became an American Foreign Service officer. Gogo joined the Red Cross and went to India, leaving her little dog, Popcorn, with her mother.

Schiap took Popcorn for long walks every day through Central Park and the streets of New York. "I spent most evenings by myself reading," she wrote, "or with very old friends, Americans who had lived for much of their lives in France or Italy." Many months went by before Schiap received a letter from her daughter, who was stationed near the Burma front to build a club for servicemen. Gogo had become sick with amoebic dysentery and was ill for months before coming back to New York.

At two in the morning on June 4, 1944, Schiap happened to wake up and turn on the radio. "I listened to the detailed and incredible description of the Allied invasion of Normandy," she wrote. "My heart vibrated like harp-strings in the wind . . . We all had hope. We saw freedom."

On August 25, 1944, the Allies liberated Paris. On the front page of the *American Journal,* Schiap read an open letter to her from a journalist who had located her house on rue de Berri and her business at Place Vendôme. He mentioned her workers by name, and Schiap said, "I felt as if they were waving at me from a distance." At last, in the summer of 1945, she returned to Paris. She found her house "practically intact" and "went from room to room gaping" with relief. At her Place Vendôme salon, American GIs were lined up waiting to buy her signature perfumes, such as Shocking, to take home to wives and girlfriends. She was deeply touched by the devotion of her staff, who had kept the business alive during the war years.

ow Schiap's problem was: "How to start again? . . . Materials were lacking, and so were those small, utterly necessary things such as pins and needles. I had brought over so many with me, I might have been disguised as a pincushion."

During the war years, she had fallen out of touch with Paris styles. "I had not thought at all about fashion during my long stay in America," she wrote. The type of elegance she remembered from before the war was no longer fashionable. And now she faced fresh competition. A slightly younger designer named Christian Dior introduced "the New Look": softer, more romantic clothes with tiny, nipped-in waists and long, full

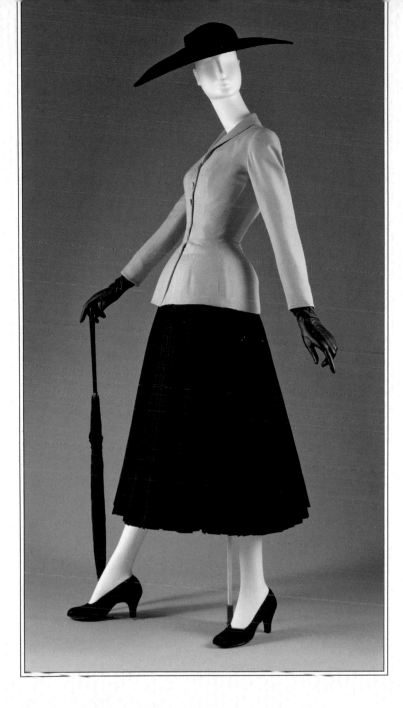

Christian Dior's "Bar" suit and jacket, which a fashion magazine editor dubbed "the New Look," 1947. After the hardships, rationing, and strict economy during World War II, women wanted to return to a simpler life, especially in new and more feminine clothes that accentuated their curves. Dior's black skirt and tailored jacket are dull compared to Schiap's bright colors, unique buttons, zippers, embroidery, and imaginative themes.

ballerina skirts. After suffering rationing during wartime, Dior luxuriated in using yards and yards of fabric for a single dress. Women loved it.

Another French designer who might have inspired the New Look was Jacques Fath. His glamorous, sumptuous ball gowns with tiny waists were worn over huge crinolines and began the "crinoline craze." Elsa's adventurous designs, meant to shock and excite, had lost their appeal.

A Spanish designer, Cristóbal Balenciaga, addressed the New Look by eliminating the waistline. He brought out the sack dress, the chemise, and the baby doll dress.

Meanwhile, in the United States, Claire McCardell promoted the American Look. She used natural, common fabrics—calico, gingham, and denim—for mix-and-match separates that were mass-produced and inexpensive.

Despite the competition, Schiap forged on and put together playful new collections: the Talleyrand silhouette in 1945, named for the eighteenth-century French politician; the Broken Eggshell silhouette in 1947, with jagged edges; and the Grasshopper collection in 1952, featuring cellophane collars that projected outward like little wings.

Schiap also kept concocting crazy headwear. There was the Robin Hood hat. Then a red satin evening cap covering one half of the face with a peephole for the eye. And a straw hat covering the whole face with a cellophane window to see through. None of these caught on, however, the way her earlier designs had. Not even a shocking-pink velvet beret decorated with sequins and pearls. In an interview she said, "The daring is gone. No one can dream anymore."

The harsh realities of the war had influenced the change in styles. Schiap's staff of workers looked worried and worn-out. Some of the men who had not died in combat were not yet back from prison camps. Her models were too thin because they had not had enough to eat. Schiap said, "I did not immediately realize that the sort of elegance we had known before the war was now dead."

So Schiap began to focus on simpler, more practical designs. Commercial airlines were the up-and-coming new way to travel, replacing the steamship. She anticipated the need for these travelers to carry their luggage, rather than have porters handle it; with this in mind she designed her Commuter's Bag. Weighing barely ten pounds, it could hold six dresses, a coat, and three folding hats. The *New York Times* described it as "the largest handbag known to woman."

"I was still a dreamer," she wrote, "and I con-tinued to have a vision of women dressed in a practical yet dignified and elegant way." Schiap brought out her most spectacular ensemble for spring 1947: a shocking-pink taffeta and black crepe jacket embroidered in jet-black beads forming three-dimensional flowers and tied in back with a huge bow like a bustle. The combination of hot pink and black was her all-time favorite. And in 1950 she designed a shocking-pink gown with an embroidered short bolero, the style she had popularized in the 1930s. Her evening wear remained beautiful, but sales plummeted. Schiap was in serious financial trouble, in danger of going bankrupt.

"(Women) should dare to be different."

In 1952, she designed her last set of costumes for a movie, *Moulin Rouge*, named for a famous nightclub in Paris. The film was about the artist Henri de Toulouse-Lautrec. Schiap created the wardrobe for the star of the movie, Zsa Zsa Gábor, and she copied the clothes directly from Toulouse-Lautrec's posters. The movie won two Oscars and was enormously popular, but it did not help Schiap's business.

In February 1954, Schiap presented her farewell collection, which introduced *bateau* (boat-shaped) necklines. Her couture business had lost so much money that she was forced to declare bankruptcy and close her salon at Place Vendôme. However, she managed to keep her art- and antiques-filled mansion with the money earned from her perfumes and accessories, which still sold extremely well in America and Europe.

On a train trip to Italy, she reflected on her life. She thought about other professions she might have chosen. Sculptor? Painter? Writer? Actress? Cook?

"I remained with the fact that many years ago I had become a maker of dresses," she concluded. "I had overcome great difficulties, enjoyed immense success . . . The presentation of fashion was a work of art, a truly beautiful thing."

In her autobiography, she listed "twelve commandments" for women and wrote, "Ninety percent are afraid of being conspicuous and of what people will say . . . They should dare to be different."

Schiap designed this shocking-pink gown and embroidered bolero in 1950.

Epilogue

When Schiap retired in 1954, she focused on enjoying friends and family. Gogo had given birth to daughters Marisa, in 1947, and Berinthia (nicknamed Berry, like her father), in 1948. Schiap adored her granddaughters. At her mansion on rue de Berri, she gave children's tea parties for them and made them matching dresses in ruby-colored velvet with shocking-pink sashes. Marisa grew up to be a top fashion model and actress, and Berry became a fashion photographer for *Vogue* magazine.

Schiap divided her time between her luxurious mansion on rue de Berri and a small white house she had bought in the old fishing village of Hammamet, Tunisia. While still in good health, she traveled and attended concerts, the theater, and fashion openings. Her work greatly influenced younger designers—French, British, Italian, and American.

Schiap outlived her rival, Chanel. But after suffering several strokes, Schiap was confined to bed. Wearing exquisite embroidered lingerie and scented with Shocking perfume, she rested against heart-shaped shocking-pink pillows. On November 13, 1973, she died in her sleep. She was eighty-three.

Fashion designer Yves Saint Laurent said, "Madame Schiaparelli trampled down everything that was commonplace . . . Her imagination knew no bounds. She alone could have given to a pink the nerve of a red. A pink that went on to devour everything in its path . . . a neon pink, an unreal pink. Shocking pink!"

Author's Note

Who decides what is beautiful? The subject is forever controversial. We are bombarded with so-called ideals of beauty in fashion magazines, on TV, and in movies. Ads for makeup and skin-care and hair-care products appear everywhere. Diet fads often lead to illness. Many people feel that our culture places too much emphasis on physical appearance. Even back when Elsa Schiaparelli was working as a fashion designer and setting trends, she understood that what mattered most was feeling good about oneself and having confidence. And that is what she did and promoted in her own life and work.

WHERE TO SEE THE WORK OF ELSA SCHIAPARELLI

Museums throughout the world have collected and preserved Elsa Schiaparelli's designs, from swimsuits and sweaters to gloves and gowns. These are some of the places where her work can be seen:

North America
Goldstein Museum of Design, University of Minnesota, St. Paul, Minnesota. www.goldstein.design.umn.edu
Metropolitan Museum of Art, The Costume Institute, New York, New York. www.metmuseum.org/about-the-museum/museum-departments/curatorial-departments/the-costume-institute
Museum at FIT (Fashion Institute of Technology), New York, New York. www.fitnyc.edu/museum.asp
Phoenix Art Museum, Arizona Costume Institute, Phoenix, Arizona. www.arizonacostumeinstitute.org
Philadelphia Museum of Art, Costume and Textiles Collection, Philadelphia, Pennsylvania. www.philamuseum.org
Royal Ontario Museum, Toronto, Ontario, Canada. www.rom.on.ca/en
Salvador Dalí Museum, St. Petersburg, Florida. thedali.org

Europe
Filmmuseum Berlin, Marlene Dietrich Collection, Berlin, Germany. www.deutsche-kinemathek.de/en
Musée de la Mode et du Textile, Les Arts Décoratifs, Paris, France. www.lesartsdecoratifs.fr/en/about-us/collections
Musée Galliera (formerly Musée de la Mode de la Ville de Paris), Paris, France. www.palaisgalliera.paris.fr/en
Peggy Guggenheim Collection, Venice, Italy. www.guggenheim-venice.it

Victoria and Albert Museum (V&A), Fashion Collection, London, United Kingdom. www.vam.ac.uk

Australia
National Gallery of Australia, Decorative Arts and Design, Parkes, Canberra. nga.gov.au/home/default.cfm

Asia
The Kyoto Costume Institute, Kyoto, Japan. www.kci.or.jp

SCHIAPARELLI'S FASHION FIRSTS

This book intentionally concentrates more on Elsa Schiaparelli's contribution to the world of fashion and art rather than on aspects of her personal life. She introduced many "firsts" that are still popular today:

- Bolero jackets
- Brand-name scarves
- Buttons shaped as decorative accessories
- Boutiques
- Carry-on bags
- The color hot pink
- Fashion runway shows
- Jumpsuits
- Leopard-print booties
- Lounging pajamas
- Rayon and synthetic fabrics for fashionable clothing
- Shocking perfume in a bottle shaped like the female form (Mae West's!)
- Shoulder bags
- Themed collections
- Trompe l'oeil sweaters with bows, collars, and designs knitted in
- Wedge shoes
- Wraparound dresses and skirts
- Zippers as a design element (and that also functioned)

SELECT ARTWORKS THAT INSPIRED SCHIAPARELLI

Georges Braque, *Still Life on a Table* (collage), 1914

Georges Braque, *Still Life with Tenora* (*The Clarinet*) (cubist collage), 1913

Georges Braque, *Violin and Pipe*, *"Le Quotidien"* (collage), 1913

Jean Cocteau, *Adam and Eve* (drawing), 1959

Jean Cocteau, *Le Testament d'Orphée*, a film (poster), 1960

Jean Cocteau, *Les Cyclades* (marble sculpture), 1926

Salvador Dalí, *Lobster Telephone*, 1936

Salvador Dalí, *Venus de Milo with Drawers*, 1936

Meret Oppenheim, fur-covered bracelet, 1936

Pablo Picasso, *Bird Cage and Playing Cards* (oil painting), 1933

Pablo Picasso, *Guitar* (collage with newspaper), 1914

SELECT ARTWORKS THAT SCHIAPARELLI INSPIRED

Salvador Dalí, *Night and Day Clothes of the Body* (diptych), 1936

Meret Oppenheim, *Object*, popularly known as *Le Déjeuner en Fourrure* ("Luncheon in Fur") (fur-lined teacup, saucer, and spoon), 1936

Pablo Picasso, *Portrait of Nusch Éluard*, 1937

Man Ray, *Hands Painted by Picasso* (photograph), 1935

Man Ray, photograph of Schiaparelli's head superimposed on a plaster torso, to illustrate "L'Age de la Lumière" (The Age of Light) in art periodical *Minotaure*, December 12, 1933

Man Ray, *Le Beau Temps* (a phrase he understood to mean "the good times") (oil on canvas), 1939

Man Ray, drawing for *Les Mains Libres* (poems by Paul Éluard), 1937

BIBLIOGRAPHY

Books

Baudot, François. *Elsa Schiaparelli*. New York: Universe Publishing, 1997.

———. *Fashion & Surrealism*. New York: Assouline Publishing, 2002.

Baxter-Wright, Emma. *(The Little Book of) Schiaparelli*. London: Carlton Books, 2012.

Berenson, Marisa. *Marisa Berenson: A Life in Pictures*. New York: Rizzoli, 2011.

Blum, Dilys E. *Shocking! The Art and Fashion of Elsa Schiaparelli*. Philadelphia: Philadelphia Museum of Art, 2003.

Chaney, Lisa. *Coco Chanel: An Intimate Life*. New York: Penguin Books, 2012.

Dalí, Salvador. *The Secret Life of Salvador Dalí*. New York: Dover Publications, 1993.

de la Haye, Amy, and Shelley Tobin. *Chanel: The Couturiere at Work*. Woodstock, New York: The Overlook Press, 1994.

Friedel, Robert. *Zipper: An Exploration in Novelty*. New York: W.W. Norton & Company, Inc., 1996.

Grenier, Catherine. *Salvador Dalí: The Making of an Artist*. Paris: Flammarion, 2013.

Madsen, Axel. *Coco Chanel: A Biography*. London: Bloomsbury, 2009.

Matthews, Elizabeth. *Different like Coco*. Cambridge, Massachusetts: Candlewick Press, 2007.

Néret, Gilles. *Dalí*. Los Angeles: Taschen, 2011.

Picardie, Justine. *Coco Chanel: The Legend and the Life*. New York: It Books, HarperCollins, 2010.

Schiaparelli, Elsa. *Shocking Life: The Autobiography of Elsa Schiaparelli*. London: V&A Publications, 2007. Originally published in 1954.

Secrest, Meryle. *Elsa Schiaparelli: A Biography*. New York: Alfred A. Knopf, 2014.

Stuart, Amanda Mackenzie. *Empress of Fashion: A Life of Diana Vreeland*. New York: HarperCollins, 2012.

Volk, Patricia. *Shocked: My Mother, Schiaparelli, and Me*. New York: Alfred A. Knopf, 2013.

Watt, Judith. *Vogue on: Schiaparelli*. London: Quadrille Publishing, 2012.

White, Palmer. *Elsa Schiaparelli: Empress of Paris Fashion*. London: Aurum Press Limited, 1996.

Catalogs

Schiaparelli and Prada: Impossible Conversations. New York: The Metropolitan Museum of Art, 2012.

Christie's. *Collection Personnelle d'Elsa Schiaparelli*. Auction: January 23, 2014, 9 avenue Matignon, 75008, Paris, France.

Articles

Flanner, Janet. "Profiles: Comet." *New Yorker*, June 18, 1932.

Menkes, Suzy. "Schiaparelli for Sale." *New York Times*, November 18, 2013.

SOURCE NOTES

page 4: "bright pink begonias." Elsa Schiaparelli, *Shocking Life: The Autobiography of Elsa Schiaparelli* (London: V&A Publications, 2007), p. 2.

page 4: "the color flashed . . . A shocking color." Schiaparelli, p. 89.

page 6: "Never was a name less appropriate." Schiaparelli, p. 2.

page 6: "Schiap was an ugly child." Schiaparelli, p. 5.

page 7: "as ugly . . . sister was beautiful." Schiaparelli, p. 6.

page 7: "If she could make . . . throat, ears, mouth." Schiaparelli, p. 6.

page 7: "She felt . . . nearly suffocate . . . the chief . . . turn her into a beauty." Schiaparelli, p. 6.

page 7: "flying machine." Richard McLanathan, *Leonardo da Vinci* (New York: First Impressions, Harry N. Abrams, Inc., 1990), p. 66.

page 7: "threw herself into space." Schiaparelli, p. 9.

page 7: "He would . . . long visit." Schiaparelli, p. 14.

pages 7–9: "He liked me . . . on my cheek." Schiaparelli, p. 13.

page 9: "I spent long . . . everything on." Schiaparelli, p. 13.

page 9: "This was not . . . edged with lace." Schiaparelli, p. 17.

page 9: "The fact that . . . revolted me." Schiaparelli, p. 17.

page 9: "as a punishment." Schiaparelli, p. 20.

page 9: "hate the strict rules . . . take her home." Schiaparelli, p. 20.

page 10: "this was the golden opportunity." Schiaparelli, p. 24.

page 10: "This is . . . going to live!" Schiaparelli, p. 24.

page 10: "Persian silhouette." "Paul Poiret: King of Fashion." FIDM Museum Blog, accessed August 19, 2009, http://blog.fidmmuseum.org/museum/2009/08/my-entry-1.html.

page 11: "a small sensation." Schiaparelli, p. 25.

page 11: "It was . . . first couturiere's failure." Schiaparelli, p. 25.

page 12: "listened spellbound . . . communion of ideas." Schiaparelli, p. 26.

page 12: "But they failed . . . a registry office." Schiaparelli, p. 26.

page 12: "ultra-modern painter." Schiaparelli, p. 31.

page 12: "immediately fell . . . continual gurgling." Schiaparelli, p. 30.

page 13: "could hardly walk . . . like a crab." Schiaparelli, p. 35.

page 13: "I reeled under the blow." Schiaparelli, p. 36.

page 13: "If I have . . . a liking for it." Palmer White, *Elsa Schiaparelli: Empress of Fashion* (London: Aurum Press Limited), p. 44.

page 13: "beautiful things." Schiaparelli, p. 37.

page 14: "Ladies come to . . . not a dressmaker." "Paul Poiret: King of Fashion," FIDM Museum Blog.

page 14: "While my friend . . . been made for you." Schiaparelli, p. 38.

page 14: "I cannot . . . anything anywhere." Schiaparelli, p. 38.

page 14: "invent . . . but an art." Schiaparelli, p. 42.

page 14: "Women at that . . . and jumpers." Schiaparelli, p. 43.

page 15: "butterfly bow . . . a black [back]ground." Schiaparelli, p. 43.

page 15: "mad idea . . . third, sensational." Schiaparelli, p. 43.

page 15: "created a . . . one immediately." Schiaparelli, p. 43.

page 16: "an artistic masterpiece." Dilys E. Blum, *Shocking! The Art and Fashion of Elsa Schiaparelli* (Philadelphia: Philadelphia Museum of Art, 2003), p. 13.

page 16: "chic bowknot sweater." Blum, p. 13.

page 16: "became very daring." Schiaparelli, p. 44.

pages 16–17: "pierced hearts . . . skeleton sweater." Schiaparelli, p. 46.

page 17: "Schiaparelli . . . POUR LE SPORT." Schiaparelli, p. 45.

page 17: "fish wriggling on the stomach." Schiaparelli, p. 47.

page 18: "It was our . . . so young." Schiaparelli, p. 41.

page 18: "For those who . . . bathing suits." Schiaparelli, pp. 178–179.

page 18: "This proved . . . over the world." Schiaparelli, p. 47.

page 18: "who stirred interest . . . being well dressed." Schiaparelli, p. 52.

page 19: "The body . . . in a building." Schiaparelli, p. 46.

page 19: "like the leaves of a four-leaf clover." Schiaparelli, p. 47.

page 19: "as an *arpette* . . . alive, and creative." Schiaparelli, p. 45.

page 20: "She had even . . . were delighted." Schiaparelli, p. 50.

page 20: "She was between . . . for a month." Schiaparelli, p. 50.

page 20: "real collection . . . in the train . . . dared to hope." Schiaparelli, p. 50.

page 20: "At last . . . vastly successful." Schiaparelli, p. 50.

page 20: "one of the rare creators." White, p. 66.

page 20: "All the laws . . . to be news." Schiaparelli, p. 49.

page 21: "got so tired . . . thought of it." Schiaparelli, p. 49.

page 21: "could do . . . look attractive." Schiaparelli, p. 67.

page 22: "All this in . . . from scratch." Janet Flanner, "Profile: Comet," *New Yorker*, June 18, 1932, accessed August 25, 2014, http://www.newyorker.com /magazine/1932/06/18/comet.

page 22: "She is ranked . . . Paris dressmaking." Flanner, "Profile: Comet."

page 22: "that Italian who's making clothes." Blum, p. 125.

page 22: "The walls seemed . . . growing crowds." Schiaparelli, p. 64.

page 22: "the world's center . . . wealth in Paris." Schiaparelli, p. 65.

page 22: "At the sight . . . passing a cemetery." Schiaparelli, p. 48.

pages 22–23: "wore on . . . like a newspaper . . . silk and cotton." Schiaparelli, p. 68.

page 23: "I had always . . . my colleagues." Schiaparelli, p. 61.

page 23: "I had them . . . startling materials." Schiaparelli, p. 62.

page 23: "My staff was courteous and capable." Schiaparelli, p. 62.

page 23: "Always on time, five minutes early." White, p. 79.

page 24: "the very first . . . over the world." Schiaparelli, p. 65.

page 24: "It became . . . as a Paris landmark." Schiaparelli, p. 65.

page 24: "shocking pink . . . among my friends." Schiaparelli, p. 90.

page 24: "set the fashion world spinning." White, p. 152.

page 25: "The success . . . and immediate." Schiaparelli, p. 90.

page 25: "Dare to be different." Schiaparelli, p. 211.

page 26: "We worked . . . definite themes." Schiaparelli, p. 91.

page 26: "stupefied by . . . horrible blue uniform." Schiaparelli, p. 96

page 27: "I went as often . . . to be picked up." Schiaparelli, p. 97.

page 27: "I saw it . . . lucky number . . . middle of Paris." Schiaparelli, p. 93.

page 27: "beloved paintings . . . books, books, books." Schiaparelli, p. 94.

page 27: "fantastic imagination" and "daredevil approach." Schiaparelli, p. 66.

page 27: "Schiaparelli is . . . a devil's laboratory." White, p. 179.

page 27: "Not only . . . on evening clothes." Schiaparelli, p. 66.

page 27: "Why don't you . . . evening dresses?" Amanda Mackenzie Stuart, *Empress of Fashion: A Life of Diana Vreeland* (New York: HarperCollins, 2012), p. 112.

page 27: "Artists took . . . they do now." Schiaparelli, p. 69.

page 27: "a sense of . . . supported and understood." Schiaparelli, p. 69.

page 27: "Dalí was . . . famous pictures." Schiaparelli, p. 90.

page 28: "desk suit." White, p. 140.

page 29: "had the courage to wear it." Schiaparelli, p. 90.

page 29: "mad." Salvador Dalí. *The Secret Life of Salvador Dalí* (New York: Dover Publications, 1993), p. 313.

page 29: "Fantasy combined . . . of fashion." Dalí, p. 314.

page 29: "defiantly . . . for eccentricity." Schiaparelli, p. 90.

page 32: "Why don't you . . . unique materials?" Stuart, p. 354 (note for p. 112).

page 32: "He was a . . . almost a fanatic." Schiaparelli, p. 91.

page 33: "Not one . . . look like." Schiaparelli, p. 91.

page 33: "the most riotous and swaggering collection." Schiaparelli, p. 91.

page 33: "The mannequins [models] . . . through the salons." Blum, p. 169.

page 33: "It was just . . . hysteria and tension." Axel Madsen, *Coco Chanel: A Biography* (London: Bloomsbury, 2009), p. 219.

page 34: "Gogo was going places." Schiaparelli, p. 98.

pages 34–35: "Dear Gogo . . . Don't give in to it." White, p. 112.

page 35: "lived an enchanting . . . beautiful clothes." Schiaparelli, p. 99.

page 36: "of the immense . . . declaration of war." Schiaparelli, p. 100.

page 36: "The little black . . . no tailors." Schiaparelli, p. 104.

page 36: "had to leave . . . necessary to her." Schiaparelli, p. 104.

pages 36–37: "poured in to . . . French Mechanized Transport Corps." Schiaparelli, p. 103.

page 37: "was soon . . . six-wheeled truck." Schiaparelli, p. 104.

page 37: "Monday—no meat . . . *toujours l'amour* [always love]." Schiaparelli, p. 106.

page 37: "visiting their . . . near the front." Schiaparelli, p. 106.

page 37: "but we did . . . into production." Schiaparelli, p. 107.

page 37: "The Americans . . . should leave." Schiaparelli, p. 107.

page 37: "She chose to be American." Schiaparelli, p. 40.

page 37: "On the ship . . . young American." Schiaparelli, p. 107.

page 39: "A black cloud enveloped the city." Schiaparelli, p. 107.

page 39: "My work-people . . . into tears." Schiaparelli, p. 109.

page 39: "for the country of her adoption." Schiaparelli, p. 109.

page 39: "I was not . . . a great craft." Schiaparelli, p. 13.

page 39: "Will you . . . come back?" Schiaparelli, p. 110.

page 39: "a huge . . . beaming shyly." Schiaparelli, p. 112.

page 39: "American hospitality . . . and exhilarating." Schiaparelli, p. 55.

page 39: "particular creative work." Schiaparelli, p. 112.

page 39: "But in spite . . . American young man." Schiaparelli, p. 115.

page 40: "It was no . . . in France." Schiaparelli, p. 115.

page 40: "I was still . . . something to eat." Schiaparelli, p. 121.

page 40: "The minister knew . . . in danger." Schiaparelli, p. 122.

page 40: "My own situation . . . and more difficult." Schiaparelli, p. 121.

page 41: "I found . . . on the spot." Schiaparelli, p. 122.

page 41: "who had startled . . . a staircase." Schiaparelli, p. 135.

page 41: "All this was new to me." Schiaparelli, p. 136.

page 41: "filled her . . . of self-respect." Schiaparelli, p. 137.

page 42: "unanimous and . . . for action." Schiaparelli, p. 139.

page 42: "I spent most . . . or Italy." Schiaparelli, p. 141.

page 42: "amoebic dysentery." Schiaparelli, p. 145.

page 42: "I listened to . . . saw freedom." Schiaparelli, p. 151.

page 42: "I felt as . . . a distance." Schiaparelli, p. 151.

page 42: "practically intact." Schiaparelli, p. 154.

page 42: "went from room to room gaping." Schiaparelli, p. 155.

page 42: "How to start . . . as a pincushion." Schiaparelli, pp. 156–157.

page 42: "I had not . . . stay in America." Schiaparelli, p. 158.

page 43: "crinoline craze." "French Fine Art Fashion Prints Collection: Jacques Fath, 1912–1954 Fashion Designer." 1951 Photo Shoot Spring Crinoline Ball Gowns, accessed August 25, 2014, http://headtotoefashionart.com/jacques-fath-1912-1954.

page 44: "The daring . . . anymore." White, p. 216.

page 44: "I did not . . . was now dead." Schiaparelli, p. 158.

page 44: "the largest handbag known to woman." Blum, p. 250.

page 44: "I was still . . . elegant way." Schiaparelli, p. 159.

page 45: "I remained with . . . beautiful thing." Schiaparelli, p. 206.

page 45: "Ninety percent . . . to be different." Schiaparelli, p. 211.

page 46: "Madame Schiaparelli . . . unreal pink. Shocking pink!" White, pp. 12–13.

IMAGE CREDITS

Jacket and case: Schiaparelli, photographed by George Hoyningen-Huene, 1932. Hoyningen-Huene / *Vogue*, © Condé Nast; **page 5:** Schiaparelli, "Dinner Jacket," Philadelphia Museum of Art; **page 6:** From *Shocking Life* by Elsa Schiaparelli, copyright 1954 by E. P. Dutton & Co., Inc. Used by permission of Dutton, a division of Penguin Group (USA) LLC; **page 8:** © The Metropolitan Museum of Art. Image source: Art Resource, NY; **page 10:** Library of Congress, LC-USZ62-100840; **page 11:** © The Metropolitan Museum of Art. Image source: Art Resource, NY; **page 13:** © Man Ray Trust / Artists Rights Society (ARS), NY / ADAGP, Paris 2014; **page 16:** Schiaparelli, "Pullover Sweater," Philadelphia Museum of Art; **page 17:** Schiaparelli, "Woman's Bathing-Suit Top," Philadelphia Museum of Art; **page 19:** John Phillips / The LIFE Picture Collection / Getty Images; **page 21:** Library of Congress, LC-USZ62-64667; **page 23:** Gianni Dagli Orti / The Art Archive at Art Resource, NY. © 2014 Artists Rights Society (ARS), New York / ADAGP, Paris; **page 25:** Image courtesy of the Advertising Archives; **page 26:** Associated Press; **page 28, top:** Salvador Dalí, Fundació Gala-Salvador Dalí, Artists Rights Society (ARS), New York 2014; **page 28, bottom:** Beaton / *Vogue*, © Condé Nast; **page 29:** Schiaparelli, "Lobster Dress," Philadelphia Museum of Art; **page 30, left:** Library of Congress, LC-DIG-ppmsca-09380; **page 30, right:** Schiaparelli, in collaboration with Jean Cocteau, "Evening Coat," Philadelphia Museum of Art; **page 31, top:** Schiaparelli, "Woman's Gloves," Philadelphia Museum of Art; **page 31, bottom:** The Kobal Collection at Art Resource, NY; **page 32:** Schiaparelli, "Woman's Evening Dress," Philadelphia Museum of Art; **page 34:** Schiaparelli, "Woman's Shoes," Philadelphia Museum of Art; **page 35:** © The Metropolitan Museum of Art. Image source: Art Resource, NY; **page 38:** Image courtesy of NewspaperArchive.com; **page 40:** Schiaparelli, "Woman's Dinner Jacket," Philadelphia Museum of Art; **page 43:** © The Metropolitan Museum of Art. Image source: Art Resource, NY; **page 45:** Private Collection Photo © Christie's Images / Bridgeman Images.

ACKNOWLEDGMENTS

When I first told my editor, Howard Reeves, about my idea for a children's book on Elsa Schiaparelli, he showed interest right away. So my thanks to Howard for the pleasure of working on this project with him. At Abrams I also want to thank Orlando Dos Reis, editorial assistant; Maria Middleton for her gorgeous design; Jason Wells and Morgan Dubin in marketing; and Jen Graham, a wonderful managing editor.

Many people helped me research Schiaparelli's life and work and find images. I am grateful to Dilys Blum, senior curator of costumes and textiles at the Philadelphia Museum of Art; author Patricia Volk; Pat Frost, director of Christie's fashion department; Nicholas Nicholson, art advisor; George Nicholson, agent and friend, for his invaluable advice and insights; and my husband, Michael Rubin, for taking me to see the Palazzo Corsini, where Schiap grew up. A huge thank-you to my son Andrew Rubin for his technical assistance. And, as always, enormous thanks to my writer friends at Lunch Bunch and the Third Act for their friendship and support.

INDEX